Seasonal Crafts
Spring

RAINTREE
STECK-VAUGHN
PUBLISHERS
The Steck-Vaughn Company

Austin, Texas

Seasonal Crafts

Spring • Summer • Autumn • Winter

Published by Raintree Steck-Vaughn Publishers, an imprint of Steck-Vaughn Company

Printed in Italy. Bound in the United States
1 2 3 4 5 6 7 8 9 0 02 01 00 99 98

Picture acknowledgments:
HAGA/Britstock-IFA 26; Robert Harding 6 (A.Woolfitt); Image Bank 12, 24; Impact 14 (Simon Shepheard), Peter Sanders 8; Slide File 20; Tony Stone Worldwide 10 (Doug Armond), 22 (Paul Harris); Zefa Picture Library 4, 16, 18, 28. Cover photograph by Chris Fairclough. All other commissioned photography by Zul Mukhida. Props made by Gillian Chapman.

Library of Congress Cataloguing-in-Publication Data
Chapman, Gillian
Spring/Gillian Chapman.
p. cm.—(Seasonal crafts)
Includes bibliographical references and index
Summary:Describes some of the holidays that are celebrated around the world in spring, including Easter, Valentine's Day, Hina Matsuri, Purim, April Fool's Day, and provides instructions for a variety of related craft projects.
ISBN 0-8172-4872-2
1. Spring festivals—Juvenile Literature. [Spring festivals. 2. Festivals. 3. Holidays. 4. Handicraft.] I. Title. II. Series: Chapman, Gillian. Seasonal Crafts.
GT4504.C53   1998

394.262—dc21   97-17159
                                                                    CIP
                                                                     AC

Contents

Words that are shown in **bold** are explained in the glossary on page 31.

Arrival of Spring

△ *Trees and flowers come alive with the brilliant colors of spring.*

Spring is the season of awakening, when everything in the natural world comes to life again after the cold winter. The sun begins to warm the earth, the days get longer, and flowers and trees blossom.

Many years ago people found it hard to survive the long, harsh winters. The people of northern Europe celebrated the arrival of spring with a great festival in honor of **Eostre**, the goddess of spring. Today the name of the Christian spring holiday of Easter comes from this ancient celebration.

Spring Celebrations

Many spring holidays give families and friends the chance to celebrate together. There are big celebrations at Carnival and Easter. The Jewish festival of Purim and the Hindu festival of Holi are also times for dressing up and having fun.

Before you start:
Collect all the materials and equipment you need before you start a project. They are listed at the top of each page. An adult's help may be needed with some of the steps.

Spring Projects

There are also a number of special days, such as St. Valentine's Day, when giving cards and presents are an important part of the celebrations. This book will show you how to make cards and gifts for these occasions.

Saving Paper and Cardboard

Try to recycle as much paper and cardboard as you can especially if it has only been used on one side. Different projects will need paper of different colors and thickness, so start collecting now.

Scraps of colored cardboard and paper are used in making many of the projects. You will need only tiny pieces to decorate an animal face or a headdress, so keep even the smallest scraps.

Spring Animals

Spring is a time when new life comes into the world. The days are warmer, and animals, birds, and insects become active again, looking for mates and building nests. It is also the season of new growth, with parks and gardens full of blossoming flowers and trees.

Spring celebrations are times of hope and happiness. People give each other gifts of candy and cards, decorated with pictures of flowers, eggs, baby animals, and birds. Try making one of these animal boxes to hold your spring gifts.

Ewes with their newborn lambs can be seen in the spring. ▽

Making Animal Boxes

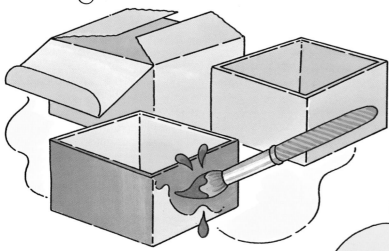

1 Find some small empty boxes, and cut off the lids and flaps. Paint them inside and out, and let them dry. △

2 Use the construction paper for cutting out shapes to decorate the boxes. Make circle-shaped heads, eyes, noses, wings, and tails. Glue them to the boxes, using the glue stick. ▽

3 Make the boxes into spring animals, such as rabbits, kittens, chicks, and lambs. Line the boxes with tissue paper, and fill them with your Easter gifts. ▽

Ramadan

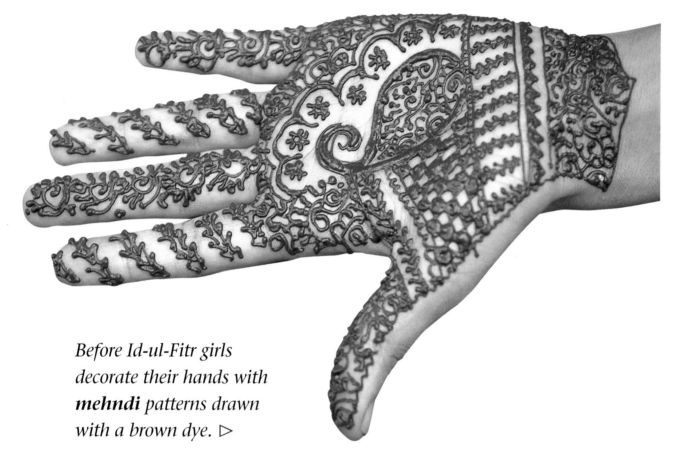

Before Id-ul-Fitr girls decorate their hands with **mehndi** *patterns drawn with a brown dye.* ▷

Ramadan is the ninth month of the Muslim year and is an important time for all Muslims. During Ramadan Muslims **devote** themselves to Allah, their God, by fasting every day between sunrise and sunset. They study the **Koran** and think about the importance of **self-discipline** and **charity**.

The festival of Id-ul-Fitr marks the end of Ramadan and is a time of joy and celebration. People attend the **mosque** for special prayers and give food and money to the poor. They wear new clothes and visit family and friends with gifts of candy and cards.

Making Mehndi Patterns

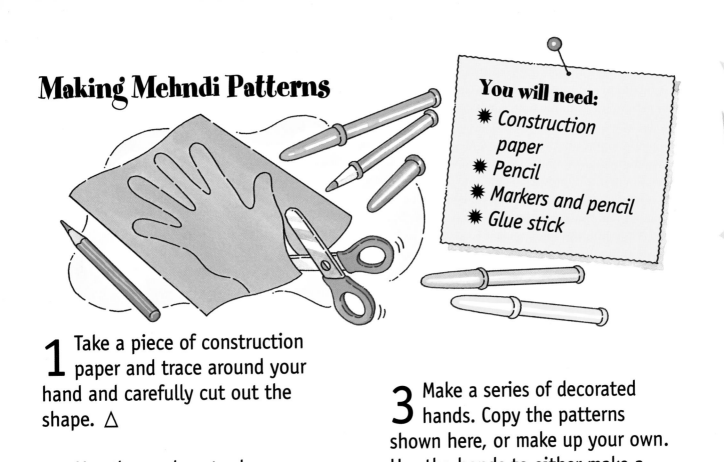

You will need:
* Construction paper
* Pencil
* Markers and pencil
* Glue stick

1 Take a piece of construction paper and trace around your hand and carefully cut out the shape. △

2 Use the markers to draw patterns on the hand shape. ▽

3 Make a series of decorated hands. Copy the patterns shown here, or make up your own. Use the hands to either make a collage or decorate a card. ▽

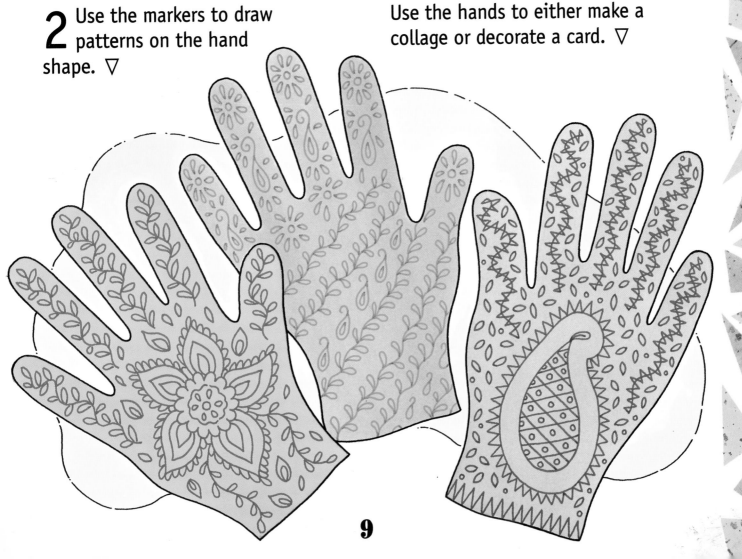

Carnival

△ *At Carnival people have the chance to dress up in bright costumes.*

Carnival is held on the Monday and Tuesday before **Lent**. In South America and the Caribbean, it is the biggest and most important festival of the year. People spend the whole year preparing spectacular costumes, masks, and headdresses for the upcoming celebration.

In New Orleans and Rio de Janeiro, huge parades are held, with the streets full of music, dancing, and steel bands. So many people take part in the street festivities that every other activity comes to a standstill.

Making a Carnival Headdress

You will need:
* Poster board (7 x 24 in.)
* Construction paper scraps for decoration
* Ruler and pencil
* Scissors
* Tape
* Glue stick

1 Draw a pencil line along the piece of poster board, 3 in. from the edge. Then cut 2 in. strips in the poster board, stopping at the line. ▽

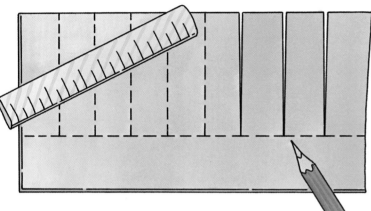

2 Use construction paper scraps to cut out the bird's face. Decorate it with eyes and a beak. Then glue the bird's face to the center strip. ▽

4 Place the headdress around your head, making sure the bird is facing the front. Ask a friend to secure the band at the back with a strip of tape. ▽

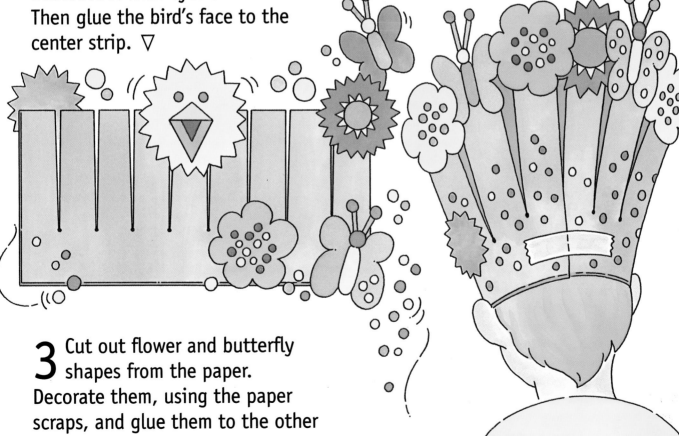

3 Cut out flower and butterfly shapes from the paper. Decorate them, using the paper scraps, and glue them to the other strips. △

11

Mardi Gras

For Christians Lent is a time of **fasting** before Easter. They remember when Jesus fasted for forty days in the desert. Mardi Gras, or Shrove Tuesday, is the day before Lent when people eat rich food. Mardi Gras is a day of fun and celebration. In Europe there are street parades and **masquerade** balls. Flower battles are also held, with people throwing flower blossoms at one another.

The first day of Lent, called Ash Wednesday, is when people used to give up foods, like meat and cheese, for the six weeks before Easter. Today most people give up their favorite kind of food.

People in clown costumes going to a masquerade ball in Italy ▽

Making a Tambourine

You will need:
- ✳ Two clean paper plates
- ✳ Pieces of ribbon
- ✳ Dried rice
- ✳ Hole punch
- ✳ Stapler
- ✳ Paints and brush
- ✳ Bells and thread

1 Put the dried rice on one of the plates, then place the second plate on top. Staple them together, making sure there are no gaps where the rice could fall out. △

2 Cut the ribbon or strips of paper into 12-in. pieces. △

4 Make some holes around the edge of the plates with a hole punch. Thread the pieces of ribbon and the bells through the holes and tie them in place. ▽

3 Paint some bright patterns on the plates and let them dry. △

St. Valentine's Day

△ *Candy in heart boxes is a popular gift on St. Valentine's Day.*

St. Valentine's Day is on February 14 of every year. It is the **custom** to send a card to someone you love on this day without signing your name. The **tradition** is believed to have started in the third century by the Bishop Valentine of Rome who was put to death for his **beliefs**. While he was in prison, he fell in love with the jailer's daughter and left a love letter for her signed "Your Valentine."

This spring holiday is now a day of fun and romance, when people have the chance to send cards, candy, and flowers to those they care about.

Making a Broken Heart Puzzle

1 Draw a heart on the piece of poster board. Then carefully cut the shape out. ▽

You will need:
✳ Piece of poster board
✳ Construction paper scraps
✳ Pencil and scissors
✳ Markers
✳ Small box or envelope

2 Use the colored markers to decorate the heart on one side. Then turn the heart over, and write a secret message on the back. △

3 Cut the heart into lots of pieces, and put them into a box or envelope. ▽

4 You can also decorate the container to match the puzzle. Then send it to someone you love on Valentine's Day. See if that person can piece together the puzzle and read your message! ▽

Hina Matsuri

The spring festival of Hina Matsuri is also known as the Peach festival. All Japanese girls are given dolls at special occasions. The dolls are beautifully dressed in silk kimonos. Some dolls are very elaborate, while others are simple—the kokeshi doll has a large, round head, no arms or legs, and is brightly painted.

At the festival of Hina Matsuri, many dolls are displayed at home, surrounded by peach blossoms. Friends of the family are invited to see them.

Dolls are displayed in Japanese homes at the festival of Hina Matsuri. ▽

Making Kokeshi Dolls

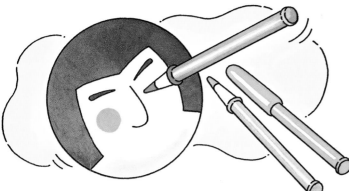

1 Use the markers to draw a face on the Ping-Pong ball. Then let it dry. △

2 Cover the cardboard tube with the wrapping paper. Attach it to the tube, using the glue stick. Tuck any extra paper into the ends of the tube. △

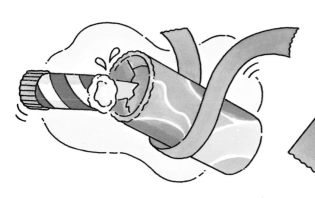

3 Dab some glue around the top edge of the tube, and attach the Ping-Pong ball head. △

You will need:
* Ping-Pong ball
* Markers
* Cardboard tube
* Wrapping paper
* Glue stick
* Scissors
* Small piece of ribbon

4 Tie the ribbon around the body to make a sash. Glue pieces of construction paper to the back of head. ▽

Purim

△ *Jewish schoolchildren dress up for the Purim holiday.*

The Jewish holiday of Purim remembers the time, many years ago, when all the Jews living in **Persia** were condemned to death. A wicked official named Haman tricked the Persian king into ordering the death of the Jews. Before they were put to death, they were saved by the king's wife, Esther.

Purim is a very happy occasion, celebrated with parties and special food. In the **synagogue** the story is read and when Haman is mentioned, everyone stamps their feet and makes noise or shakes a noisy rattle called a **grager**. The noise is to keep Haman's name from being heard.

Making a Purim Rattle

You will need:
* Construction paper
* Paints and brush
* Pencil and ruler
* Scissors
* Tape
* Colored paper strips
* Empty soda can
* Dried peas or small stones

1 Measure the width of the soda can, and cut a piece of paper long enough to wrap around the can. Then cut out a paper circle to cover the hole at the top. △

2 Paint the strip of paper with the evil face of Haman. Then paint the paper circle, and let them dry. △

3 Make sure the can is clean and dry inside. Then fill it with some dried peas or small stones. △

4 Use the tape to attach the painted paper to the side and top of the can. Tape the strips of ribbon to the bottom of the soda can. ▽

Now, when you celebrate Purim, you can shake the noisy rattle and give Haman a bad headache at the same time!

19

St. Patrick's Day

△ *On St. Patrick's Day some people dress up in green and paint traditional shamrocks on their faces.*

St. Patrick's Day, held on March 17, celebrates St. Patrick, the **patron** saint of Ireland. Around the world Irish people hold parades with marching bands and traditional dancing. It is the custom to wear a shamrock and the Irish national colors of green and gold on this day.

Legend tells how Ireland was overrun with a plague of snakes, which frightened the Irish people. St. Patrick used his powers to drive all the snakes to a cliff top and then into the sea. It is a story that **symbolizes** the power of good over evil.

Making a Wriggling Snake

First you will need to decorate the sheets of paper by splattering them with paint.

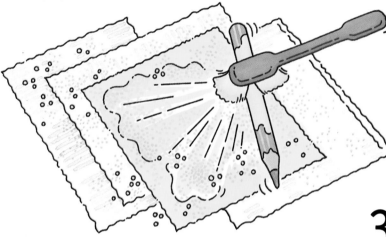

You will need:
* Construction paper
* Newspaper
* Paints and brush
* Old toothbrush
* Old pencil
* Scissors and ruler
* Glue stick
* Thread and stick

1 Place the paper on the newspaper. Dip the toothbrush in the paint, and run an old pencil across the bristles, splattering paint evenly over the paper. Let it dry. △

2 Cut the paper into 2-in. wide strips. Glue two together at right angles to each other. Fold the first strip over and crease it, then fold the second over. Keep folding one strip over the other. ▽

3 As you use up the strips, glue extra pieces to the ends. Continue adding strips and folding them to make a really long snake. ▽

4 Then glue down the head. Cut out eyes and a tongue, and glue them in place. Tie pieces of thread to each end of the snake and attach it to the stick. △

21

Holi

Holi is a Hindu Fire Festival, named after the demon goddess Holika. It is a festival of fun when people remember Krishna and the games and tricks he played. It also celebrates the arrival of spring and the success of the spring harvest. Hindus visit family and friends. They settle quarrels and look forward to the year ahead. People build huge bonfires and burn **effigies** of the goddess Holika.

During Holi colorful street processions are held, with dancing and fireworks. Houses and animals are decorated with paint, sequins, and paper streamers.

As part of the Holi festivities, people buy colored dyes to throw at passersby as a sign of good luck. ▽

Making Holi Elephants

1 Using the method explained on page 21, splatter the sheets of construction paper with different colored paint. Let it dry. ▽

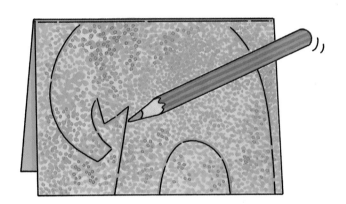

Using the method explained on page 21

You will need:
- ✹ Construction paper
- ✹ Newspaper
- ✹ Paints and brush
- ✹ Old toothbrush
- ✹ Old pencil or stick
- ✹ Scissors
- ✹ Pencil
- ✹ Glue stick

2 Fold one of the decorated sheets of paper in half. Draw a simple elephant shape on it and cut it out. Be careful not to cut the folded side. △

3 Cut out features such as ears, tusks, and a tail from the splattered paper. Glue them to the body.

Try making a blanket for your Holi elephant. Decorate it with some colored shapes. ▽

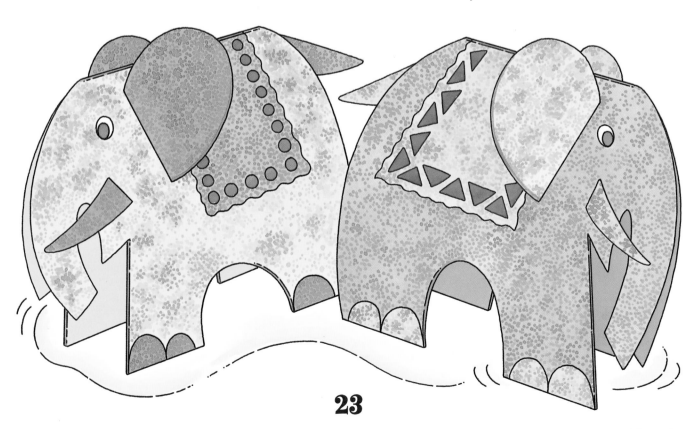

23

April Fool's Day

△ *Everyone joins in the fun on April Fool's Day.*

Celebrations have been held on April 1 for hundreds of years, but no one really knows how they started. On April Fool's Day, people play practical jokes and tricks on their friends and family. In recent years some very clever **hoaxes** have been organized by newspapers and television, which have fooled lots of people.

If you are planning any April Fool's jokes make sure they are played out before noon, otherwise the joker is the Fool!

Making Clown Figures

1 Fold the poster board in half lengthways, and cut it in two. Using the ruler and pencil, divide it into four equal sections. △

2 Draw a figure on the poster board, keeping the face on the top section of card. Draw the arms and body in the second section, the legs and knees in the third, and the feet in the bottom. △

3 Then turn the poster board over and divide it in the same way. Draw another figure in the four sections, as before. △

4 Following the lines cut the poster board into four. Punch holes in the top and bottom of each piece, and thread them together. Hang them up, and watch the clowns get really mixed up! ▽

Hana Matsuri

Hana Matsuri is a Japanese flower festival that celebrates Buddha's birthday on April 8. Buddha was born in a fragrant flowering garden, called Lumbini Grove. After his birth, he and his mother, the beautiful Queen Mahamaya, bathed in two streams that flowed from the sky. The first was cool and refreshing, and the second was warm and perfumed.

During April in Japan all the spring flowers are in bloom, and the shrines and temples are decorated with cherry blossoms.

At Hana Matsuri Japanese children sprinkle the statues of Buddha with scented tea. ▽

Making Garlands and Bouquets

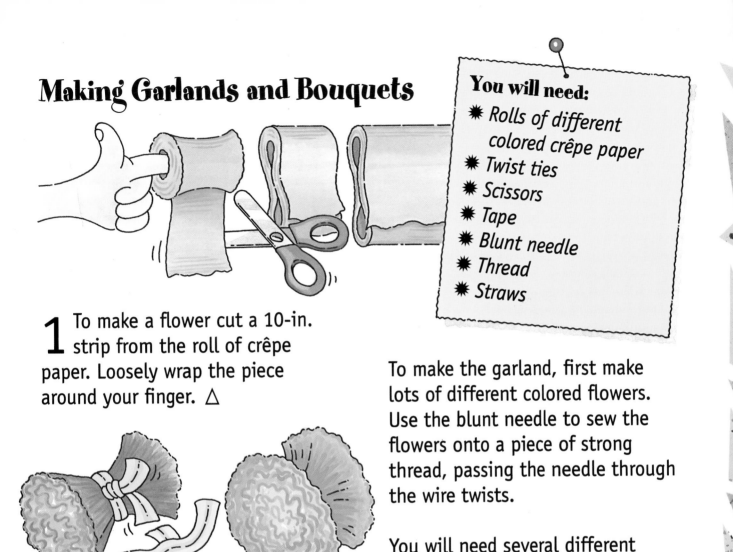

1 To make a flower cut a 10-in. strip from the roll of crêpe paper. Loosely wrap the piece around your finger. △

2 Remove the roll from your finger and secure it around the middle with a twist tie. Open the paper to make the flower. △

To make the garland, first make lots of different colored flowers. Use the blunt needle to sew the flowers onto a piece of strong thread, passing the needle through the wire twists.

You will need several different colored flowers to make a bouquet. Push the end of a plant stick into the twist tie of each flower. ▽

Easter

△ *Easter eggs symbolize the new life that comes with the spring.*

Easter is one of the most important holidays for Christians. They remember the death and **resurrection** of their **savior** Jesus Christ. The week leading up to Easter Sunday is known as Holy Week, a time of prayer with special church services. For Christians Easter Sunday is a day of happiness as they celebrate their belief that Jesus has risen from the dead.

Easter is a holiday celebrated all over the world. Families visit each another and give Easter eggs. Sometimes the Easter eggs are hidden and children hunt for them. Eggs are a special part of the Easter celebration.

Making Easter Eggs

1 Tear old newspaper into strips. Glue them over the blown-up balloon, using the diluted glue. ▽

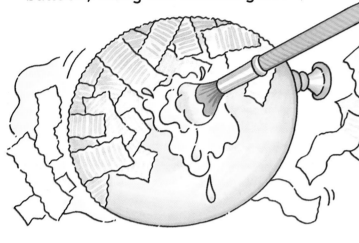

2 Cover the balloon completely with four layers of glued newspaper. Let it dry. △

3 Pop the balloon with a pin. Paint patterns on the papier mâché shape, and let it dry. Carefully cut the egg in half. △

4 Take the cardboard strip, and cut it to fit inside the bottom half of the egg. Glue it in place. The two halves of the egg should fit together. Put some tissue paper inside it, and fill it with the Easter eggs. ▽

Spring Calendar

This calendar refers only to events and festivals mentioned in this book.

Ramadan (The ninth month of the Muslim year)
January–February, but falls ten days earlier every year
Id-ul-Fitr
Festival that marks the end of Ramadan
Carnival and Mardi Gras
Celebrations that mark the beginning of Lent
Lent
Period of forty days leading up to Easter
St. Valentine's Day
February 14
Hina Matsuri (The Japanese Doll Festival)
March 3
Purim (The Jewish Festival of Lots)
Late February/early March
St. Patrick's Day
March 17
Holi (The Hindu Fire Festival)
Celebrated for 3–5 days in March
April Fool's Day
April 1
Hana Matsuri (Buddha's Birthday)
April 8
Holy Week
Christian week of prayer leading up to Easter
Easter (Christian Festival)
Late March/mid-April

Glossary

beliefs Having faith in a certain religion.

charity Giving money or gifts to the poor or needy.

custom The way certain things have always been done.

devote To love someone or something very much.

effigies Images made to look like someone.

Eostre Goddess of spring.

fasting Going without food (and sometimes water).

grager A Jewish rattle.

hoaxes Complex tricks made to confuse lots of people.

Koran Muslim Holy Book.

Lent When Christians remember Jesus' fast in the Wilderness.

masquerade To hide or disguise oneself.

mehndi Muslim (and Hindu) custom of decorating hands.

mosque A place where Muslims worship

patron Special person who cares about a particular place or people.

Persia The old name for a country in the Middle East, now called Iran.

resurrection When someone who has died is brought back to life.

savior A person who saves the lives of other people.

self-discipline To be very strict with oneself.

symbolizes Represents feelings that are difficult to describe.

synagogue A Jewish place of worship.

tradition The way things have been done over many years.

Books to Read

Corwin, Judith H. *Easter Crafts*. Danbury, CT: Franklin Watts, 1994.

Kadadula, Dilip. *Holi*. A World of Holidays. Austin, TX: Raintree Steck-Vaughn, 1997.

Kalman, Bobbie. *We Celebrate Spring*. Holidays and Festivals. New York: Crabtree Publishing Co. 1985.

MacMillan, Diane M. *Ramadan & Id al-Fitr*. Best Holiday Books. Springfield, NJ: Enslow Publishers Inc.

Penney, Sue. *Judaism*. Discovering Religions. Austin, TX: Raintree Steck-Vaughn, 1997

Index